T0194456

FROM THE *Heart* OF THE *Bishop* VOLUME II

A Moment Of Prayer

BISHOP MARY L. GUTHRIE

authorHOUSE

AuthorHouse™
1663 Liberty Drive
Bloomington, IN 47403
www.authorhouse.com
Phone: 1 (800) 839-8640

Published by AuthorHouse 06/12/2020

ISBN: 978-1-7283-6420-9 (sc)
ISBN: 978-1-7283-6419-3 (e)

Print information available on the last page.

This book is printed on acid-free paper.

Scripture taken from the King James Version of the Bible.

DEDICATION

This book is dedicated to my loving grandchildren, Jessica Walker, Jasmine Marie Kennedy, Errick Peck, Tyler Guthrie and Chase Guthrie. Each of them have a unique personality that bring so much joy to my life.

I pray this book will be an inspiration as well as encouragement to them. As they journey through the different seasons of their life, this book will be a reminder, never forget to seek God in prayer.

To my great grandsons, Ronald Reedus IV and Baby Jeremiah Kennedy, your NeNe loves you.

I also dedicate this book to my prayer partners, personal friends, and my loving family.

To my children, Pastor Tony R. Guthrie and Minister, Lady Melissa A. Peck. You have been such a blessing in my life.

To the Alumni of MLG Christian Academy School of Ministry, Indianapolis, IN. and to the Graduating Class of 2020, this book is also dedicated to each of you.

Finally, this book is dedicated to every person who need assurance to know; God does hear and answer the prayers of his people. Moreover, to the Reader of this book whose heart is touched, life is blessed, and peace is restored by the whispering prayers in this book.

ACKNOWLEDGEMENT

To My Heavenly Father, for whom I was created in His image and after His likeness.To the one who gives me power and authority; and tells me, I can do all things through Christ which strengthens me. I give you Glory and Honor for the birthing of this book.

To my Lord and Savior Jesus Christ and to the Holy Spirit that lives in me, I give you praise. It was from the depth of my spirit words began to resonate from my heart, my mind, and finally from my mouth. As a result, these words of love, gratitude, and praise became prayers to the Almighty God.

I am thankful that these prayers are now manifested in the pages of this book.

I give special honor and acknowledgment to my Family, for whom I love dearly. Your encouraging words and deeds will always be remembered and appreciated. There is nothing more special to me than my family. You are the joy of my life.

I also acknowledge, Mercy Love Grace Ministries for their contributions and support in our effort to publish this book.

To the Hermitage Inter-Faith Center, Indianapolis, IN.

And finally, I wish to acknowledge everyone who contributed, in any way, to the support of this book.

Thank You!

TABLE OF CONTENTS

FOREWORD

A *Moment of Prayer is a book of prayers that is* captivating, edifying, and invigorating! If you were inspired by her previous book "*From the Heart of the Bishop (The Journey)*", you definitely will be encouraged by "*A Moment of Prayer*". Author Bishop Mary L Guthrie has written and composed each of these Divine prayers from God in her heart to yours. The purpose of this book is to minister to your heart, bring wisdom, and reveal the spiritual connection between you and God. You will learn how to expect great things from God when you pray. Each of Bishop Guthrie's prayers in this book is an anointed sermon which lifts your spirit and takes you on a journey of hope in Him. Prayer is so vitally important and is the key that unlocks obstacles of communications between the person and God. This is one of the reasons "*A Moment of Prayer*" was written.

Bishop Guthrie is a faithful prayer warrior and a devoted Woman of God. She knows the *power* of prayer within her and its effect on others. Her prayers comfort the sick, bereaved, the saved, and the unsaved. Her prayers bring physical and spiritual healing to people. Bishop Guthrie blesses people with her prayers to include myself. I have known her for many years as a Federal employee and as one of her longtime Bible students. As Chaplain for the American Legion Women's Post #438, Indianapolis, I have grown spiritually under her teachings. A piece of advice from Bishop Guthrie is "Let your prayer requests be known unto God because He has all of the answers".

Bishop Guthrie teaches and shares her prayer life with many to include Bishops, Apostles, Pastors, Evangelists, and Ministers. She accomplishes this according to **Ephesians 4:12,** "*to equip his people for works of service,* *so that the body of Christ may be built up"*. Her prayers are so anointed people can *feel* the Holy Spirit working in her, while she prays for them. Her prayers re-enforce our purpose for life which is to demonstrate God's character and reflect His glory. No one is more qualified to write a book on prayer than Bishop Guthrie. She knows who God is, has an extraordinary in-depth knowledge of Him, and is a lifelong Christian and teacher of His word. Her prayers are very powerful and affective and fill others with love and peace.

The benefits of this book are each prayer is anointed, scriptures are supported, and opportunity is available for sharing and winning souls for Christ! Do not miss the opportunity to have this significantly important book, *"A Moment of Prayer"*, in your possession.

Mary Aurtrey
Chaplain, American Legion Women's Post #438, Indianapolis
Author, "Monthly *Chaplain's Chat*"

FOREWORD

I have known Bishop Guthrie for over 40 years and she has always personified the characteristics of a Godly, Christian woman. We were gospel singers together for ten years and traveled throughout the Midwest and the South. Hence, Bishop Guthrie was the Mistress of Ceremony for each of our programs. Every word she spoke and every song she sang demonstrated her intimate familiarity with God's Word. She revealed her thoughts, words, and advice based on the Bible. I always knew she had a calling from God to preach because that is just what she did. Subsequently, Bishop Guthrie prevailed and became one of the few women Bishops in a male dominated Christian arena. Beyond all reproach, she has remained grounded in courage and strength.

Furthermore, when Bishop Guthrie renders a prayer, she fervently grabs hold of the word of God and there is no doubt that she is being led by the Holy Spirit. One can feel the fiery words and feel the connection from the Holy Spirit and the words being transported to the hardest hearts, and people with the greatest needs.

Above all, the prayers in Bishop Guthrie's book are fervent, divine, and passionate. From the Heart of the Bishop: A Moment of Prayer is not only a book of prayers, but it is for all ages, religious denominations, or anyone seeking inner peace. As a matter of fact, even reading only one prayer the reader will not be disheartened.

To say the least, the book is a blueprint to make you cognizant of the fact that God is the architect in your life and rely on Him to be the builder of your spiritual life through prayer.

-Phyllis Barnes

INTRODUCTION

This book is a collection of prayers that express love, gratitude, and praise to our Almighty God, the one who gives life.

As you read through the pages of this book, you will be captured by the deep thoughts in my spirit that manifest the love, compassion, and obedience to God. In addition, it will also display the authority, the power and victory of God.

These prayers are designed to usher you to a place of tranquility, serenity, and rest. A calm place of total peace, where only God the Father resides.

You will discover God's faithfulness, his forgiveness, and his goodness. You will further discover God's healing, his deliverance and salvation.

It is my desire, as you read this book, that you will recognize God's power at work, see the wonders of his glory, as well as feel the presence of the Holy Spirit.

It is my hope, that you receive a divine revelation of God's love, his plan, and purpose; and decide to give Him; "A Moment of Prayer" in your life.

THE MODEL PRAYER

After this manner therefore pray ye:

Our Father which art in Heaven, hallowed be thy name.
Thy kingdom come, Thy will be done in earth, as it is in heaven.
Give us this day our daily bread.
And forgive us our debts, as we forgive our debtors.
And lead us not into temptation, but deliver us from evil:
For thine is the kingdom, and the power, and the glory, for ever.
(Matthew 6:9-13) KJV

Amen…

God's Word:

Hebrews 4:16 Let us therefore come boldly unto the throne of grace, that we may obtain mercy, and find grace to help in time of need.

1

CREATION

Most Holy and Gracious Father, I thank you for creating me in your image and after your likeness. You have made me unique and special according to your word in Gen.1:26-28.

Because of your wonderful word, I know who I am, and whose I am. I thank you for molding me into a magnificent creation.

Help me to demonstrate your character and reflect your glory, so that the world will see Jesus Christ living in me; and I will be careful to give you all the Glory, all the Honor and all the Praise.

In Jesus Name,

Amen…

God's Word:

Psalms 139:14 I will praise thee; for I am fearfully and wonderfully made: marvelous are thy works; and that my soul knoweth right well.

ACCEPTABLE PRAYER

Dear Heavenly Father,

Let the Words of my mouth and the Meditation of my Heart, be acceptable in thy sight, Oh Lord, my strength and my redeemer. (Psalms 19:14)

In the Name of Jesus,

Amen...

God's Word:

Romans 12:1 I beseech you therefore brethren, by the mercies of God, that ye present your bodies a living sacrifice, holy, acceptable unto God, which is your reasonable service.

PRAYER OF BLESSINGS

Most Holy and Gracious Father, I thank you for the many blessings you have bestowed upon my life. You are my keeper, my helper and my healer. You are my protector, my provider, and my peace. You are the source of life.

When I was hurting, you comforted me, when I was sick you healed me, when I was weak you strengthened me and when I couldn't see my way, you made a way.

Thank you God for good health, a sound mind, and your loving spirit living in me.

I thank you that you have blessed my coming in and my going out. I am graced with the blessings of your unconditional love, your perfect peace and your unspeakable joy.

I'm thankful that I am abundantly blessed. I give You all the glory honor and praise.

In the Precious Name of Jesus,

Amen…

God's Word:

Deuteronomy 28:8 The Lord shall command the blessing upon thee in thy storehouses, and in all that thou settest thine hand unto; and he shall bless thee in the land which the Lord they God giveth thee.

PRAYER OF BLESSINGS

Heavenly Father;

I thank you for New Vision, Fresh Anointing, and Greater Works.

I thank you for showing me your will, your plan and your purpose for my life.

You have instilled in me a desire to serve. Even before I knew the possible potential within me, before knowing my spiritual gifts, or aware of your power in me; you placed in my heart a desire to serve others. I now know, you were preparing me for your divine plan.

Father, I thank you for my passion, for your will, your plan, and your purpose.

I am truly grateful to you, for blessing me with new vision, your fresh anointing, and greater works for the Kingdom of God.

In the Mighty Name of Jesus,

Amen…

God's Word:

John 14:12 Verily, verily, I say unto you, He that believeth on me, the works that I do shall he do also; and greater works than these shall he do; because I go unto my Father.

PRAYER OF COMFORT

Dear Heavenly Father, I ask that you comfort your people who are suffering due to life's many struggles. I kneel in pray on behalf of my sisters and brothers that are hurting today. There are those who are hurting due to the lost of a loved one, others may be struggling from oppression, sickness or financial crises. Whatever the situation may be, I ask that you move right now on their behalf.

You are the sovereign God. You are in control of everything.

Your word tells us in Romans 8:28 "And we know, that all things work together for good to them that love God"

Father, I ask that you help your people during these troublesome times. Help them to turn to you for comfort and strength; and I pray, they find peace and rest in you. In Jesus Name.

This is your humble Servant's prayer.

Amen…

God's Word:

Psalms 121:1 I will lift up mine eyes unto the hills, from whence cometh my help. My help cometh from the Lord, which made heaven and earth.

PRAYER OF CONFESSION

Heavenly Father, According to your word in Romans 10:9-10 "That if thou shalt confess with thy mouth the Lord Jesus, and shalt believe in thine heart, that God hath raised him from the dead, thou shalt be saved."

For with the heart man believeth unto righteousness; and with the mouth confession is made unto salvation.

Father, I confess, believe, and acknowledge the death, burial and resurrection of your Son Jesus Christ; and I receive my salvation in Him.

I am now the righteous of God.

In Jesus Name,

Amen...

God's Word:

John 1:12 But as many as received him, to them gave he power to become the sons of God, even to them that believe on his name.

COVENANT PRAYER

Heavenly Father, I thank you for your covenant that you made with humanity as revealed in the scripture. This covenant that was made many years ago between you and the Israelites, your chosen people, was the promise to protect them if they were faithful and kept your law.

I thank you that you are the same yesterday, today and will be forever more.

Today, we still have your promises, but because of your Son, Jesus Christ who sacrificed His life on the cross, we now have a new covenant. The covenant of your Grace.

Because of your covenant, I choose to have no other gods before you, I choose to love you with all my heart and to love my Neighbor. I choose to praise and worship you and you only in spirit and in truth. And, I choose to keep your commandments, your statue, and your judgment. Thank you God for this new covenant, your unmerited favor. I thank you for your Covenant of Grace.

This is your humble Servant's prayer.

Amen…

God's Word:

Hebrews 9:15 And for this cause he is the mediator of the new testament, that by means of death, for the redemption of the transgressions that were under the first testament, they which are called might receive the promise of eternal inheritance.

DECREE

Father in Heaven,

I Decree and Declare that I am Healed, Healthy and Whole.

I Decree and Declare that my Body is Healed, My Heart is Healthy, and my Mind is Sound.

I Decree and Declare, I have the Activity of all my Limbs; and I am Completely Whole.

In the Precious and Powerful Name of Jesus,

Amen...

God's Word:

Mark 9:23 Jesus said unto him, if thou canst believe, all things are possible to him that believeth

DECLARATION

Dear Heavenly Father,

I Declare your Riches in Glory, the Wealth of the Wicked, and Prosperity.

I Declare that you will supply all of my needs, according to your riches in Glory.

I Declare that the wealth of the wicked, is laid up for the righteous;

I Declare that whatsoever things are done for the sake of the Gospel shall Prosper.

I Declare Prosperity for Christian ministry, spiritual care and Kingdom building.

In the Mighty and Majestic Name of Jesus,

Amen...

God's Word:

Phil 4:19 But my God shall supply all your need according to his riches in glory by Christ Jesus.

PRAYER OF DELIVERANCE

Father God, I come before you right now acknowledging you, as my deliverer. You have delivered me from the bondage of sin, from the fear of failure, the fear of rejections, from depression and so much more.

I am delivered from the strongholds of the enemy, (Satan) who comes to steal, and kill and destroy. I confess Jesus Christ as my savior; and I am under the precious blood of Jesus. Because of the cross, I am free from the snares of the enemy.

I speak deliverance in my life.

In Jesus Name,

Amen…

God's Word:

Psalms 107:20 *He sent his word, and healed them, and delivered them from their destructions.*

PRAYER OF FAITH

Dear Lord,

I thank you for Shepherding Anointing, For Preaching Power; And Leadership Wisdom.

You are the Almighty God, A Wonderful Councilor, The Prince of Peace.

You are The Everlasting Father.

Amen...

God's Word:

Philippians 4:13 *I can do all things through Christ which strengtheneth me.*

PRAYER OF FAITH

Heavenly Father,

I stand in agreement with your word and your promises, that says;

I have what your word says I have; power and authority over all the enemy.
I can do what your word say I can do; all things through Christ which strengthens me.
I am who your word says I am; that I am fearfully and wonderfully made.

I proclaim that your word is a lamp unto my feet; and a light unto my pathway.

Your word have I hide in my heart that I might not sin against thee.

I am thankful for all the promises written in your word. By faith, I believe and receive these promises and the power of your Word.

In the Matchless Name of Jesus,

Amen…

God's Word:

Isaiah 40:8 The grass withers, the flower fades, but the word of our God shall stand forever.

FAVOR

Dear Heavenly Father, I am so grateful for your favor upon my life.

You continue to shower down your bountiful blessings upon me over and over again.

I know there were times when I fell short of your word, but you forgave me and embraced me with your love. Help me not to take your gifts for granted, but to show my love and gratitude to you for all the many blessings you have bestowed upon me.

You have poured out physical blessings, financial blessings, and all spiritual blessings in my life; day after day after day. What a Wonder You Are.

Father I thank you for your bountiful blessings; and your divine Favor upon me.

In Precious Name of Jesus,

Amen…

God's Word:

Psalms 84:11 *For the Lord God is a sun and shield: the Lord will give grace and glory; no good thing will he withhold from them that walk uprightly.*

FEAR

Father God, I thank you for being my Shepherd. You are the one who watches over me day and night. You are the one who protects me from the wiles of the evil one, and you are the one who comes to my rescue when I'm in trouble.

When the pressures of life get me down and I feel afraid, you have promised in your word, you will never leave me. I now have your assurance that I am not alone. You are with me. You are my hope, my help, and my God.

I will walk in faith and not in fear.

In the Mighty Name of Jesus,

Amen…

God's Word:

Isaiah 41:10 Fear thou not; for I am with thee: be not dismayed; for I am thy God: I will strengthen thee; yea, I will help thee; yea, I will uphold thee with the right hand of my righteousness.

PRAYER OF FORGIVENESS

Almighty and Everlasting Father. The God of Abraham, Isaac and Jacob, I come before you in the Name of Jesus, asking that you forgive me of my sins, transgressions and iniquities. Please forgive me of my sinful words, thoughts, deeds and actions.

I confess my sins before you and ask for wisdom and guidance of your Holy Spirit.

Father, your word says, if we confess our sins, you are faithful and just to forgive us of our sins, and cleanse us from all unrighteousness.

I thank you for justification, (the complete forgiveness and the righteousness of God). I am completely forgiven and in right standing with you; the Father. In Jesus Name.

This is your Servants Prayer.

Amen…

God's Word:

Psalms 32:5 I acknowledged my sin unto thee, and mine iniquity have I not hid. I said, I will confess my transgressions unto the Lord; and thou forgavest the iniquity of my sin.

PRAYER OF HOPE

Most Holy and Gracious Father,

It is in you that I live, move and have my being. When everything around me is in chaos; and it seems that there is no hope, you said; come unto me, all ye that are weary and heavy laden and I will give you rest.

Father God I know that I can find peace, rest and hope in you.

I thank you that I don't have to worry with what tomorrow will bring, because the hope that I have is in you. Therefore, I will set my mind and my future on the hope of glory, which is Christ Jesus my solid rock.

Amen...

God's Word:

Romans 12:12 *Rejoicing in hope; patient in tribulation; continuing instant in prayer.*

PRAYER OF HEALING

Most Holy and Gracious Father, I thank you for being my healer.

You are the one who heals my heart, when it is hurting from the loss of a loved one.
You are the one that heals my spirit, when it is wounded from the hurt of persecution.
You are the one who heals my body, when it is afflicted with pain, sickness and disease.

Because of the blood of Jesus that was shaded on the cross, the Bible declares; By His Stripes, We Are Healed.
Therefore, I claim healing in my Mind, Spirit, and Body.

I rebuke depression, persecution, pain, and disease; and I speak God's healing in my life, in the Name of Jesus.

I am completely healed by the blood of Jesus that has power over all sickness, affections and disease. God is my healer; and, I AM HEALED.

In the Mighty, Matchless, Magnificent, Majestic and Marvelous Name of Jesus,

Amen...

God's Word:

Isaiah 53:5 But He was wounded for our transgressions, He was bruised for our iniquities; the chastisement for our peace was upon Him, and by His stripes we are healed.

18

PRAYER OF HUMILITY

Father God,

I humble myself under your mighty hand, that you may lead, guide and direct me for the work of the ministry.

Let thy will be done in my life, as it is in Heaven.

My heart, mind, soul and spirit says yes to your will; and to your way.

I am your servant, your vessel, the one you have chosen, anointed and ordained for Christian ministry. I humbly bow before you; and thank you, for using me for your Glory.

In the Precious Name of Jesus,

Amen…

God's Word:

James 4:10 Humble yourselves in the sight of the Lord, and he shall lift you up.

INTERCESSION

Father In the Name of Jesus, I intercede right now on behalf of all those who are struggling, oppressed, hurting and in dismay.

You know every heartache, pain and struggle that your people are going through in this life.

God, you are omniscient, omnipotent, and omnipresent. You are all knowing, all powerful, and you are everywhere at the same time. Please stretch forth your hand of mercy upon us right now.

I ask that you calm the storms, and move in these circumstances. I know that you can and I believe that you will. Now Father, I thank you for hearing and answering this prayer.

In the Mighty, Precious, and Powerful Name of Jesus,

Amen…

God's Word:

I Timothy 2:1 I exhort therefore, that first of all, supplications, prayers, intercessions, and giving thanks, be made for all men.

LIBERATION

Most Holy and Gracious Father, I thank you that I am liberated by your word.

It is written in Matthew 5:43-48

Ye have heard that it hath been said, thou shalt love thy neighbor, and hate thine enemy. But I say unto you, love your enemies, bless them that curse you, do good to them that hate you, and pray for them which despitefully use you, and persecute you;

That ye may be the children of your Father which is in heaven: for he maketh his sun to rise on the evil and on the good, and sendeth rain on the just and on the unjust.

For if ye love them which love you, what reward have ye? Do not even the publicans the same? And if ye salute your brethren only, what do ye more than others? Do not even the publicans so? Be ye therefore perfect, even as your Father which is in heaven is perfect.

In the Mighty Name of Jesus,

Amen...

God's Word:

Romans 12:20-21 Therefore if thine enemy hunger, feed him; if he thirst, give him drink: for in so doing thou shalt heap coals of fire on his head. Be not overcome of evil, but overcome evil with good.

PRAYER OF LOVE

Almighty God, I thank you that Jesus Christ is our perfect example of your love; and that you have sent your Holy Spirit to help us show this love to one another.

I am grateful for your unconditional love to me. I realize there were times in my life when I didn't deserve it, but because of your mercy and compassion, you continued to pour out your unwavering love. Please help me to show the same compassion and love to others.

You said in your word, thou shalt love thy neighbor as thyself. Therefore, I choose to love my neighbor, I choose to love my enemies, and I choose to love the Lord my God.

Love is patient and kind. Love is not jealous, it does not brag, and it is not proud. Love is not rude, is not selfish, and does not get upset with others. Love does not count up wrongs that have been done. Love takes no pleasure in evil but rejoices over the truth. Love patiently accepts all things. It always trusts, always hopes, and always endures. Love never ends.

Thank you God for the spirit of love; and that your love is manifesting in my life today.

In Jesus Name,

Amen...

God's Word:

John 13:34 *A new commandment I give unto you, that ye love one another; as I have loved you, that ye also love one another.*

PRAYER OF PETITION

Dear God, I come boldly to the thrown of grace praying for the Family, the Children, every Church, and all the Leaders. I humbly ask that you bless your people everywhere.

I come before you praying for the sick, the homeless, the backslider, and all those who are in bereavement.

Your word says, by prayer and supplication with thanksgiving, let our request be made known unto you.

I pray for those behind prison bars; for sinners who need a savior; and for the whole Nation.

I ask that you heal the sick, you save the sinners, you delivery the backslider, and you heal our Land. In the Name of Jesus.

By faith, I believe it is already done; and I thank you Lord for answering this prayer.

In Jesus Name,

Amen...

God's Word:

Philippians 4:6 *Be careful for nothing; but in every thing by prayer and supplication with thanksgiving let your requests be made known unto God.*

PRAYER OF PETITION

Most Holy and Gracious Father,

I ask that you comfort me when I am lonely,
That you walk with me when I need a friend.
I ask that you keep me when I am hurting,
And help me when I'm weak and I have lost my way.

In the Mighty Name of Jesus,

Amen...

God's Word:

Mark 11:24 Therefore I say unto you, what things soever ye desire, when ye pray, believe that ye receive them, and ye shall have them.

PRAYER OF POWER

Most Holy and Gracious Father,

You have ordained and anointed me with your spiritual gifts for the perfecting of the Saints, the work of the ministry and for the edifying of the body of Christ. I speak power and authority over anything that would hinder the building of your Kingdom.

I am in agreement with your word that you have given me power according to Luke 10:19.

I know that I have power to do greater works in the Kingdom. Power to obey your word, to keep your commandments, to rise above negativity and power over the adversary.

Father, I thank you for your power that is working in my life.

In the Name of Jesus, Son of the Living God,

Amen...

God's Word:

Ephesians 3:20 Now unto him that is able to do exceeding abundantly above all that we ask or think, according to the power that worketh in us.

PRAYER OF PRAISE

I will bless the Lord at all times, his praises shall continue be in my mouth. My soul shall make her boast in the Lord: the humble shall hear thereof, and be glad. O magnify the Lord with me, and let us exalt his name together. (Psalm 34:1-3)

Father, I come into your presence with praise and thanksgiving in my heart.

I will praise you with my whole heart, I will praise you with the fruit of my lips. I will praise you with the clapping of my hands, with singing and with a dance. I will forever praise the name of the Lord. You are worthy of all our praise.

I thank you for one more day to give you one more praise.

In the Precious and Powerful Name of Jesus,

Amen…

God's Word:

Psalms 150:6 *Let every thing that hath breath praise the Lord, Praise ye the Lord.*

PRAYER OF PROTECTION

Heavenly Father, I thank you for being my dwelling place. You are my shelter in the time of storms. When the enemy sets hidden traps against me, I am protected under the blood of Jesus. When the strong winds of life is blowing and the waves are ragging, you are my safe place.

Father, I know that I can take shelter under your Almighty Arms.

It is in you that I live, move, and have my being. I thank you that I'm under the shadow of an Almighty God.

In Jesus Name,

Amen…

God's Word:

Psalms 91:1 He that dwelleth in the secret place of the most High shall abide under the shadow of the Almighty.

PRAYER OF SUPPLICATION

Most Holy and Gracious Father,

I ask for your wisdom, knowledge, and understanding to rightly divide your word of truth.

As I endeavor to teach your word, I need deeper insight and revelation from you.

I ask that you give me spiritual ears to hear, spiritual eyes to see and a spiritual mind to comprehend. I ask that you speak to me, so that I hear your voice clearly. I ask that your glory flow, so that I see your presence with me, and that your spirit abide in me, so that I will comprehend and receive revelation to the truth of your word.

Thank you for using me to help others; that I might give them the hope that's in the Promises of your Word.

In the Name of Jesus,

Amen...

God's Word:

James 1:5 *If any of you lack wisdom, let him ask of God, that giveth to all men liberally, and upbraideth not; and it shall be given him.*

PRAYER OF THANKSGIVING

Most Holy and Gracious Father, I give you glory for the wonderful things you have done in my life. You gave me your Son, Jesus Christ as my savior and redeemer; and sent your Holy Spirit to lead me along the way.

Lord I thank you…

Father, You brought me out of darkness into your marvelous light; and sent the power of your word to help, keep and strengthen me.

Lord I thank you…

You have been my friend when I was friendless, you gave me peace in times of trouble and your joy in my times of sorrow.

Lord I thank you…

You've been my healer in time of sickness, my protector from hurt, harm and danger; and you've been my provider in times of need.

Lord I thank you…

You delivered me from the schemes of the enemy and covered me under the precious blood of Jesus.

Lord I thank you…

I thank you for your mercy, love and grace. Thank you for answering my prayers, and for your miracles in my life. I give you all the glory, the honor and the praise.

In the Mighty, Matchless, Magnificent, Marvelous and Majestic Name of Jesus,

This is your humble Servant's prayer.

Amen…

God's Word:

Ephesians 5:20 *Giving thanks always for all things unto God and the Father in the name of our Lord Jesus Christ.*

VICTORY PRAYER

Dear Heavenly Father, You are the Almighty God who gives victory to those who believe and receive Jesus Christ as their Lord and Savior.

I confess that I am above and not beneath, I am the head and not the tail, I am the lender and not the borrower, I am Victorious

I confess that I am rich and not poor, I am strong and not weak, I am healthy and not lame,

I am Victorious

I am mentally, emotionally, psychologically, physically and spiritually healed, delivered and set free, I am Victorious

I confess, I no longer think negative thoughts, speak negative words, or improper actions,

I am Victorious.

Because Jesus Christ lives in me, I have victory in every area of my life. I am Victorious.

In the Name of Jesus Christ, Son of the Living God,

Amen…

God's Word:

 James 1:17 *Every good gift and every perfect gift is from above, and cometh down from the Father of lights, with whom is no variableness, neither shadow of turning.*

THE BISHOP'S PERSONAL PRAYER

Dear Heavenly Father;

I thank you for the Youth, Beauty, Good Health and Knowledge of Sarah, the Wisdom of Solomon, the Patience of Job, the Understanding of Mary the Mother of Jesus…

Thank you for the Love, Forgiveness and Compassion of our Lord and Savior Jesus Christ, the Anointing of Elijah and Elisha, the Faith of Shadrach, Meshach, and Abednego…

I thank you for the Prosperity of Joseph, the Obedience of Joshua, the Leadership of Deborah and Moses.

Thank you for the Blessings of Abraham, the Promises and Power of your Word; And for Your divine FAVOR Upon my Life.

In Jesus Name,

Amen…

God's Word:

John 15:16 Ye have not chosen me, but I have chosen you, and ordained you, that you should go and bring forth fruit, and that your fruit should remain: that whatsoever ye shall ask of the Father in my name, he may give it you.

THE HEART OF THE BISHOP
"PHRASES" TO LIVE BY:

1. Stay Focus

2. I Have No Justifiable Complaints

3. All Is Well

4. These Problems are just a Pebble in my Path for my Prosperity

5. Everybody that's With You; Is Not For You

6. What God Has for Me; It is For Me

7. Speak Lord; Your Servant is Listening

8. Working together Works

9. To God Be The Glory

10. Thank you Lord for One More Day, To Give You One More Praise

Your Words Have Power. Be careful what you speak out of your mouth.

What you speak into the atmosphere, will manifest into reality.

CONCLUSION

A. S. A. P.
(Always Say A Prayer)

It is important that we take time out of our busy schedule to have a moment with God. Our personal and intimate time with God the Father is called prayer.

It is the expression of our love, faith and gratitude, as well as giving thanks to Him for our salvation, healing and deliverance through Jesus Christ.

By prayer, we have fellowship with the Father, receive spiritual growth; and obtain victory over the enemy.

When the pressures of life have got you down, just whisper a prayer of faith,
When your family and friends are nowhere to be found, just pray a prayer of faith.
When it seems that Satan is on your track, whisper a prayer of faith, and even sometimes you feel like turning back, just pray a prayer of faith…

A. S. A. P.

<u>God's Word:</u>

I Thessalonians 5:17 *Pray without ceasing.*

PRAYER OF BLESSING ON GOD'S PEOPLE

THE LORD BLESS THEE, AND KEEP THEE,

THE LORD MAKE HIS FACE SHINE UPON THEE,

AND BE GRACIOUS UNTO THEE:

THE LORD LIFT UP HIS COUNTENANCE UPON THEE,

AND GIVE THEE PEACE.

AND THEY SHALL PUT MY NAME UPON THE CHILDREN OF ISRAEL; AND

I WILL BLESS THEM.

(Numbers 6:24-25)

God's Word:

Deuteronomy 28:6 *Blessed shalt thou be when thou comest in, and blessed shalt thou be when thou goest out.*

IN MEMORY OF PRECIOUS UPSHIRE-DUNNING

A PRECIOUS PRAYER

Good Morning, Father:
Good Morning, Jesus:
Good Morning, Holy Spirit:

Dear Heavenly Father,

I Thank You for the life of Precious Upshire-Dunning, a wonderful spirit-filled and loving Cousin. Her beautiful smile illuminated the room; and filled our hearts with love and laughter. She was full of praise, prayer and power as she ministered the word of God to others.

Her life demonstrated the love of God, and the attributes of a virtuous woman.

Her Children arise up, and call her blessed; her husband also, and he praiseth her. many daughters have done virtuously, but thou excellest them all.

Favour is deceitful, and beauty is vain: but a woman that feareth the Lord, she shall be praised. Give her of the fruit of her hands, and let her own works praise her in the gates.

(Proverbs 31:10-31)

JOURNAL

<u>JOURNAL</u>

JOURNAL

JOURNAL

ABOUT THE AUTHOR

Bishop Mary L. Guthrie is the daughter of the late Lewis and Maple Flowers of Indianapolis, IN. She is a mother, grandmother, and great-grandmother. She retired from Defense Finance and Accounting Service in Indianapolis, IN.

Bishop Guthrie is the founder and President of MLG Christian Academy School of Ministry, Indianapolis, IN. (Est. 1993). Mercy Love Grace Ministries (2002), and is the Presiding Bishop of Mercy Love Grace International Pastor's Alliance.

She attended Crispus Attucks High School, Indiana Central College in Indianapolis, IN. Apart from this, she has a certification in Christian Education, Spiritual Care, Insurance, Claims Law, and Business Administration. She was consecrated as Bishop by the Unified Inter-Denominational Churches and Universal Ministries Worldwide in 2009, and received an Honorary Doctor of Divinity.

Bishop Guthrie began her walk with the Lord at a young age of 6 years old. Her love for gospel music was the reason she began singing in the choir at her church. She served for many years as a choir director and later became a Minister of Music. As a result, she then answered her call to preach the gospel of Jesus Christ and in the interim became a Pastor and a Bishop.

She now serves as a chaplain, mentor for young ministers, instructor, life coach, President of MLG School of Ministry, and Presiding Bishop. She also conduct seminars, workshops and conferences. In addition, she is the host of the Monday Evening Prayer Ministry Broadcast.

Bishop Guthrie has received numerous awards from the State of Indiana, National Association of Female Executives, Local Community Groups, National Church Conventions, Outreach Ministry and others. Her first book From the Heart of the Bishop, The Journey was Published in 2010.

Above all, Bishop Guthrie loves the Lord and has a love for God's people. She is a dynamic teacher, a powerful preacher, a fearless prayer warrior; and a "Women of God" that is anointed to preach the message proclaiming the good news, that brings forth hope, healing, deliverance and salvation.

These are my loving grandchildren, Jasmine Marie Kennedy, (me),
Jessica Walker, Tyler Guthrie, Errick Peck and Chase Guthrie.

Printed in the United States
By Bookmasters